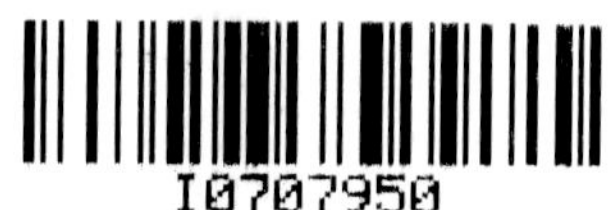

This book belongs to

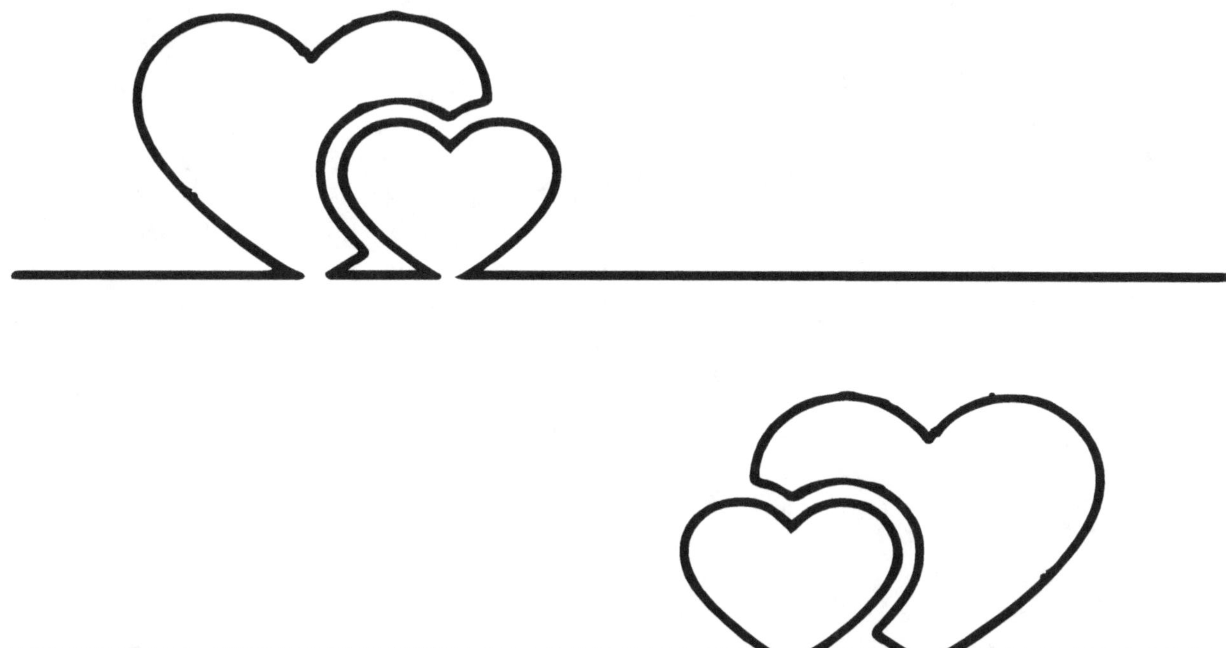

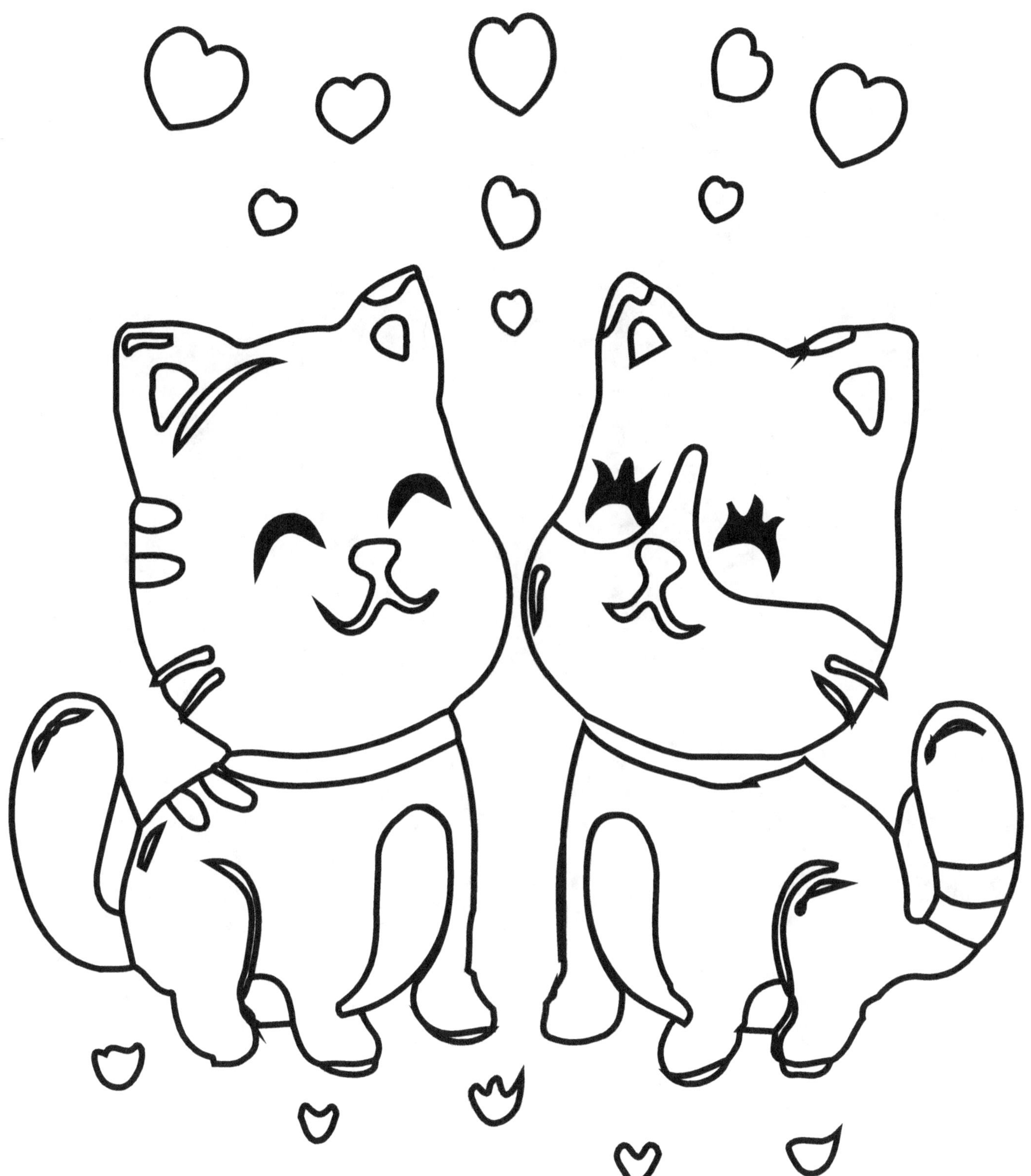

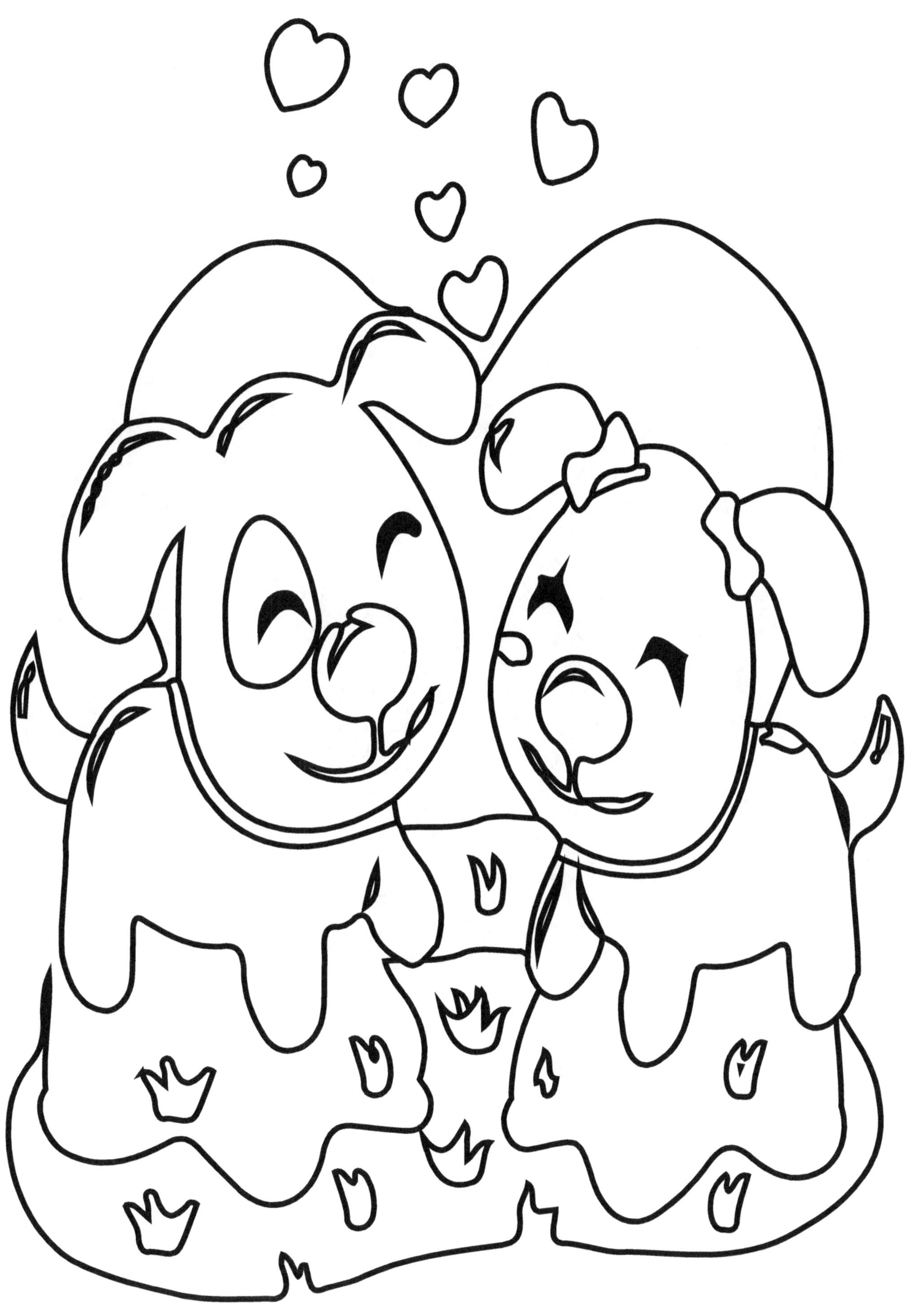

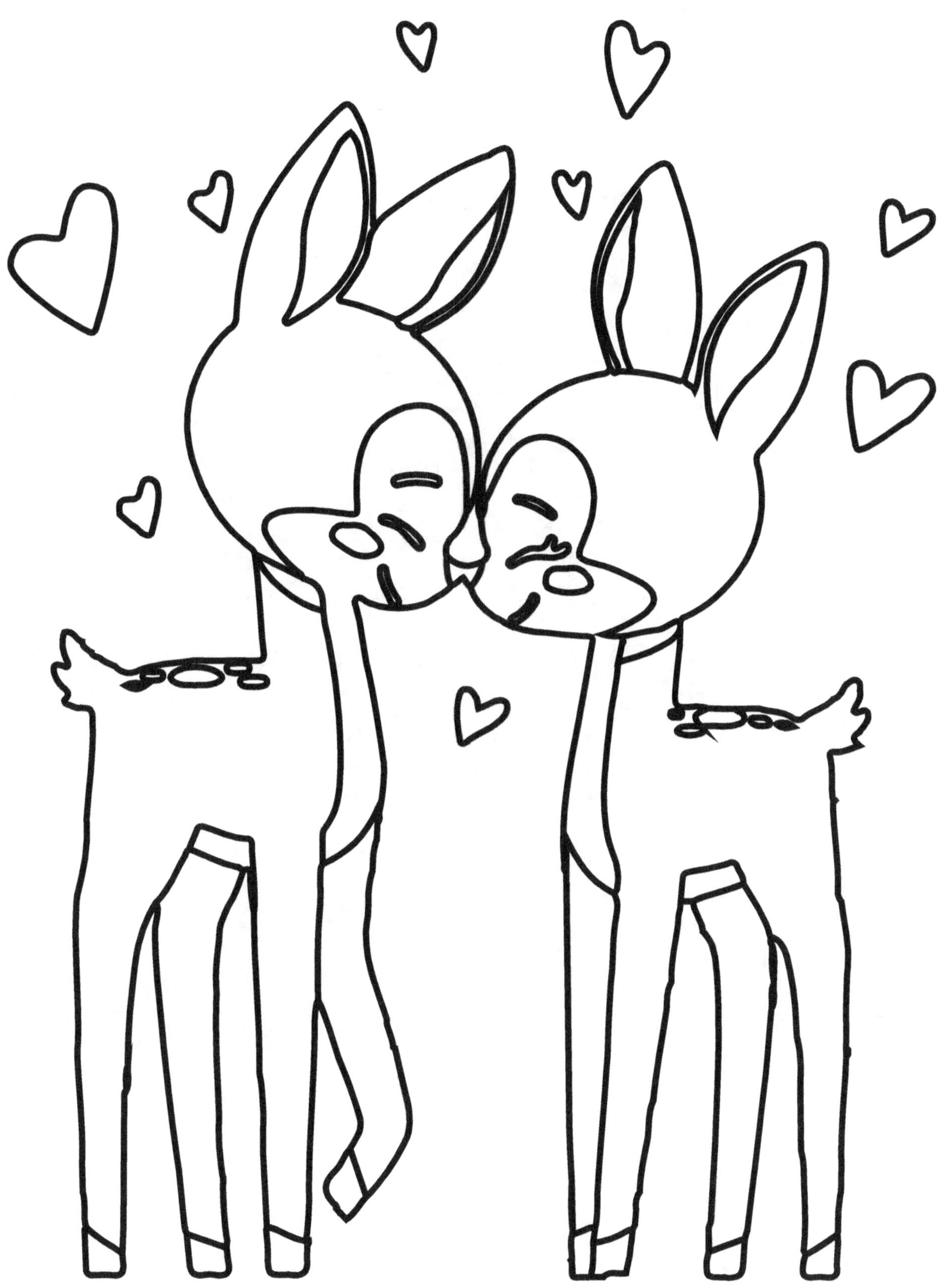

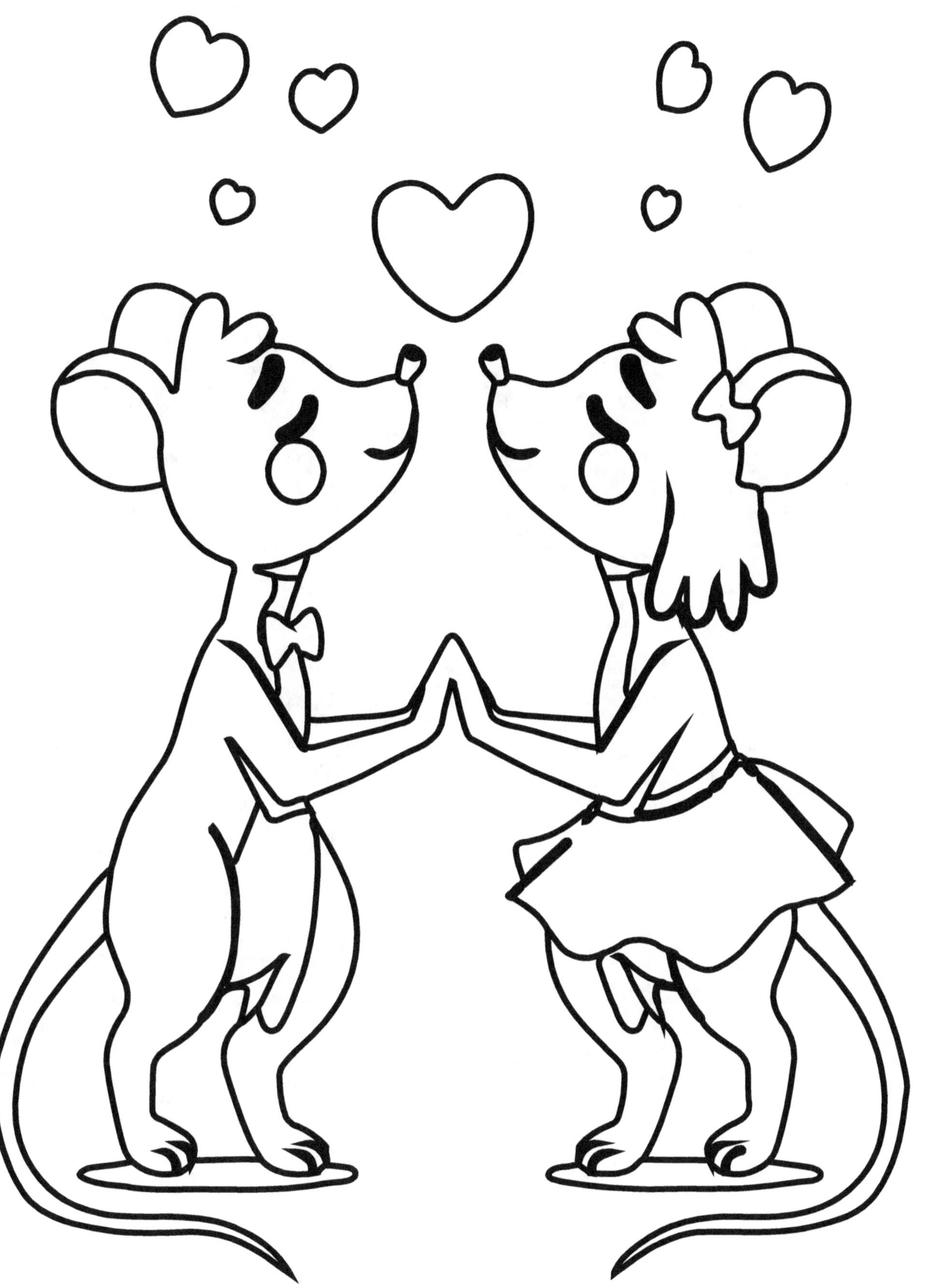

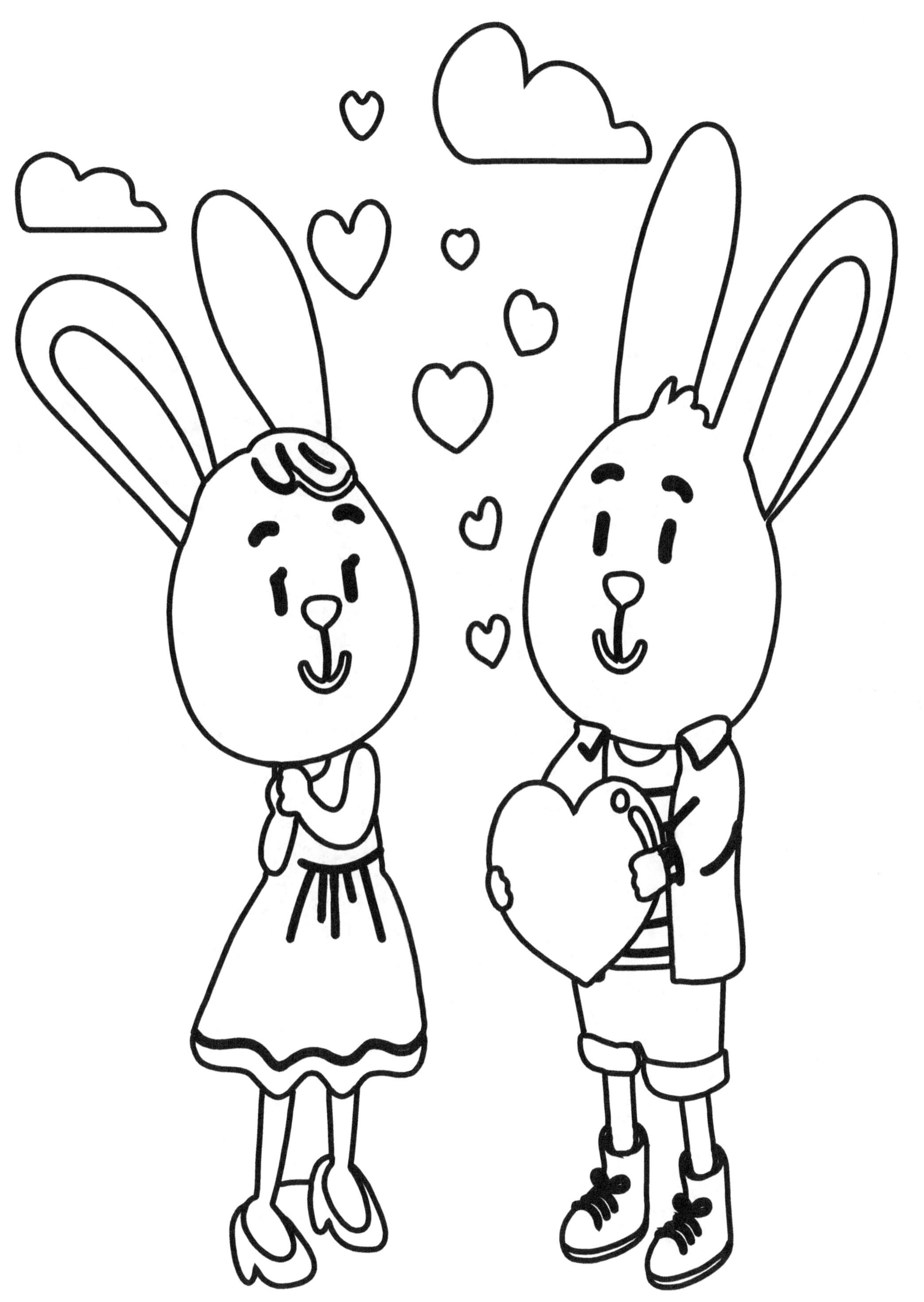

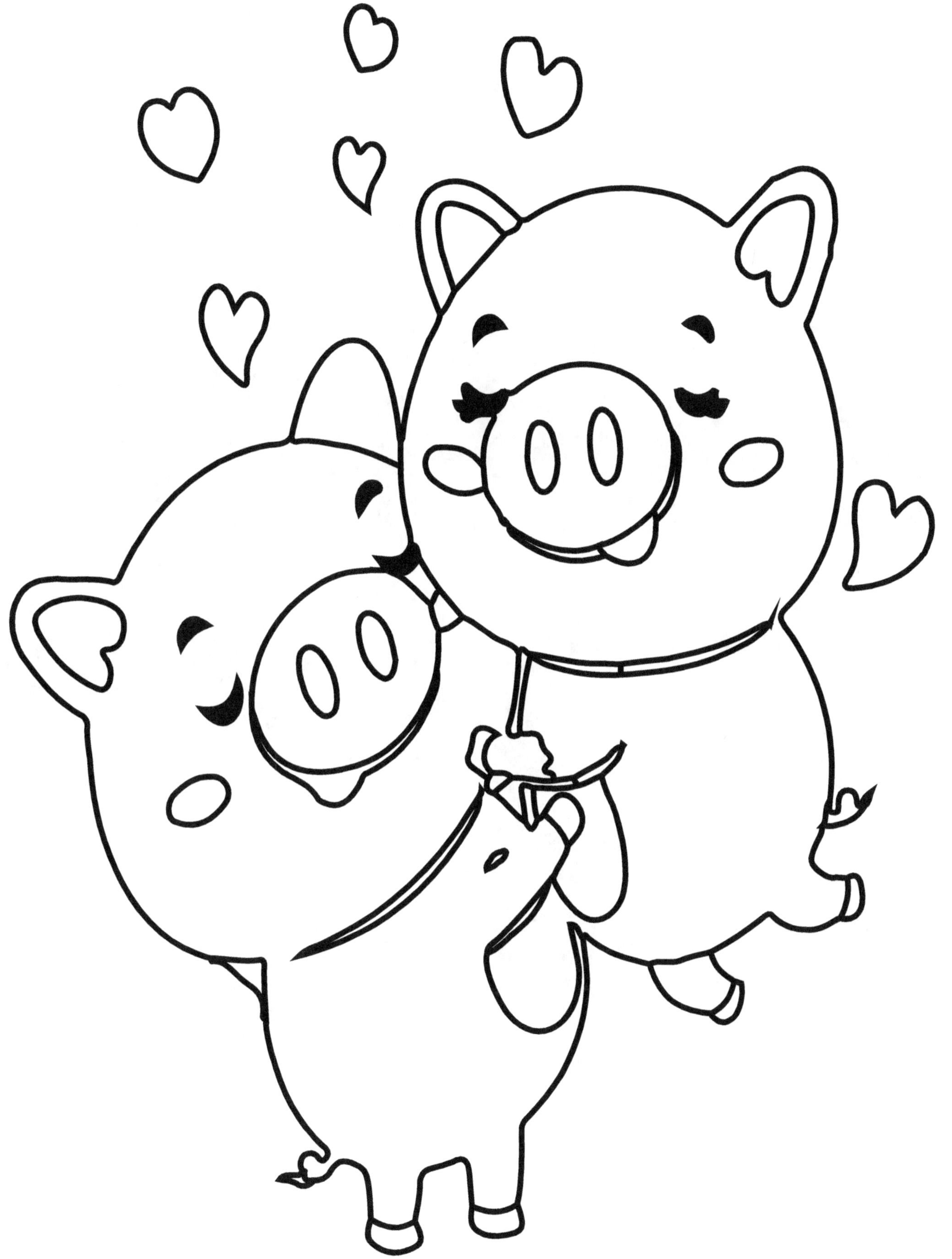

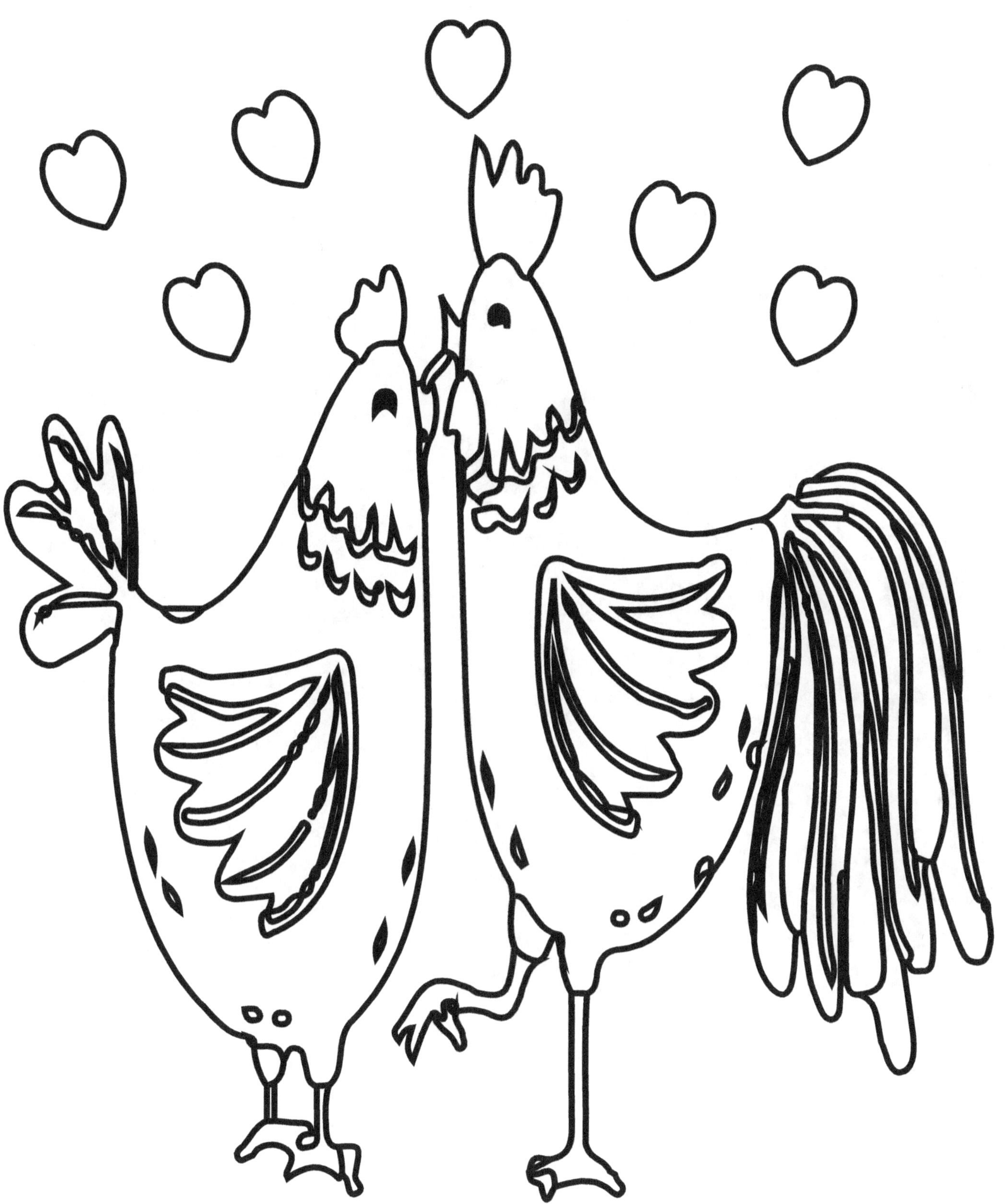

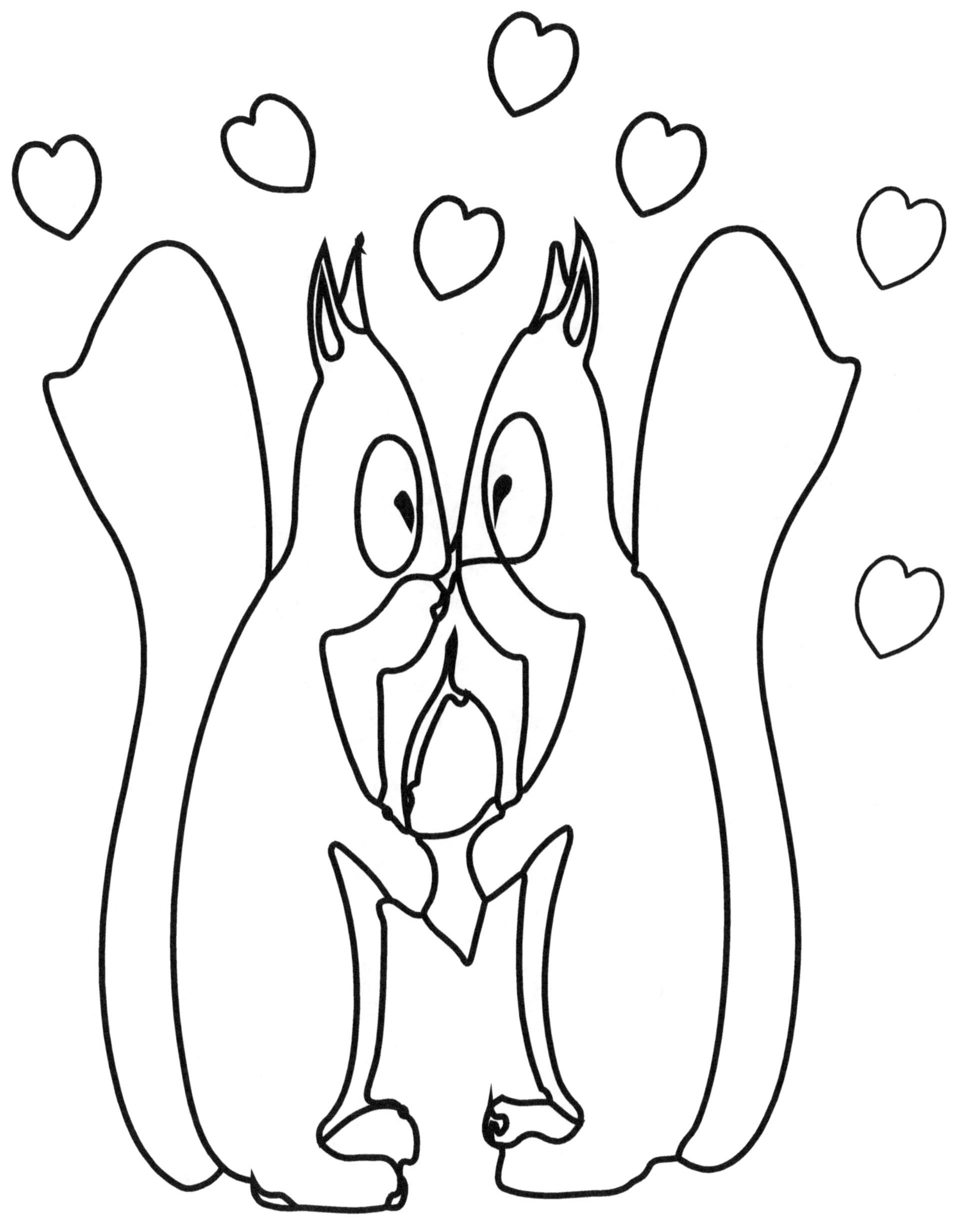

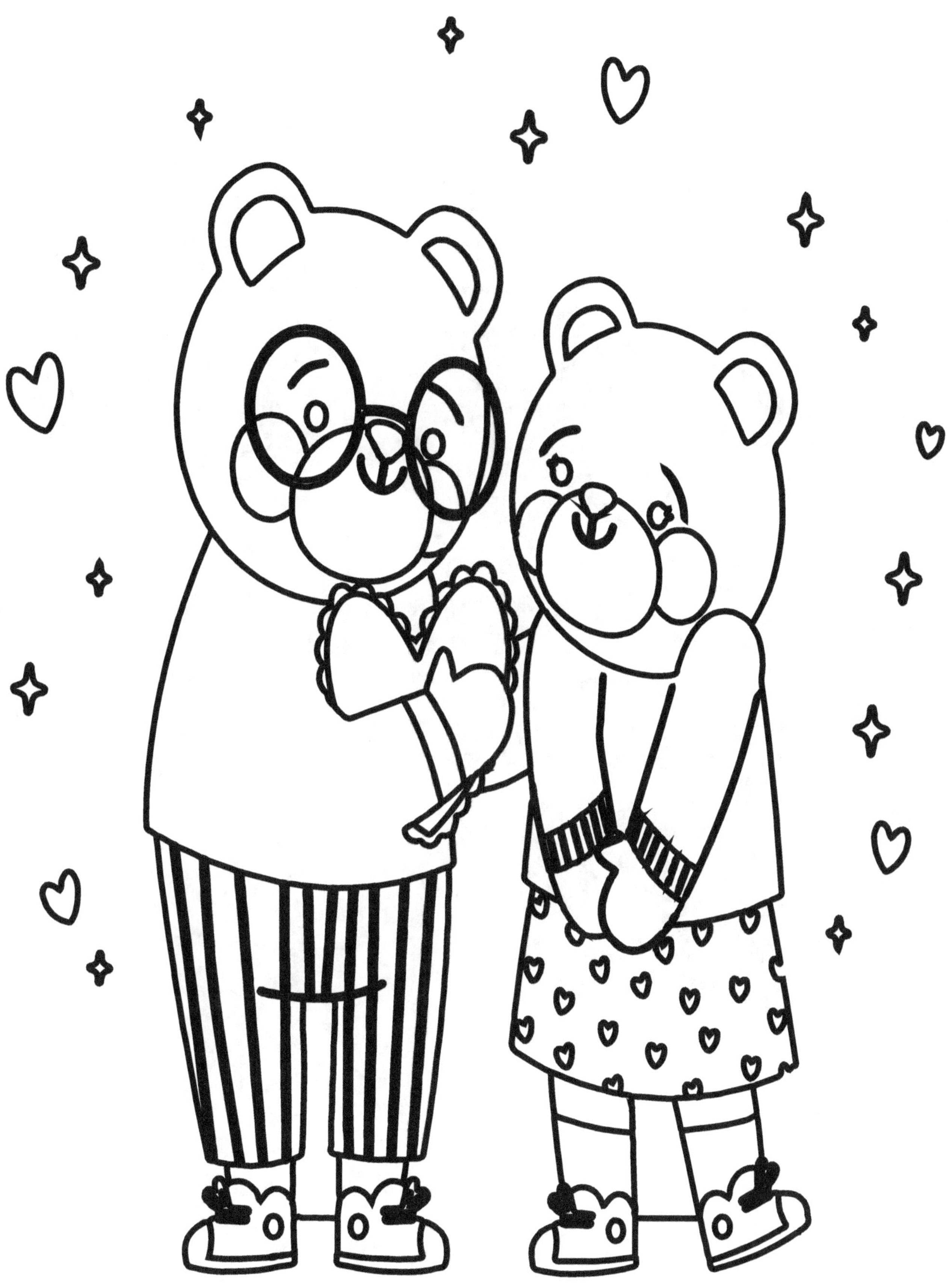

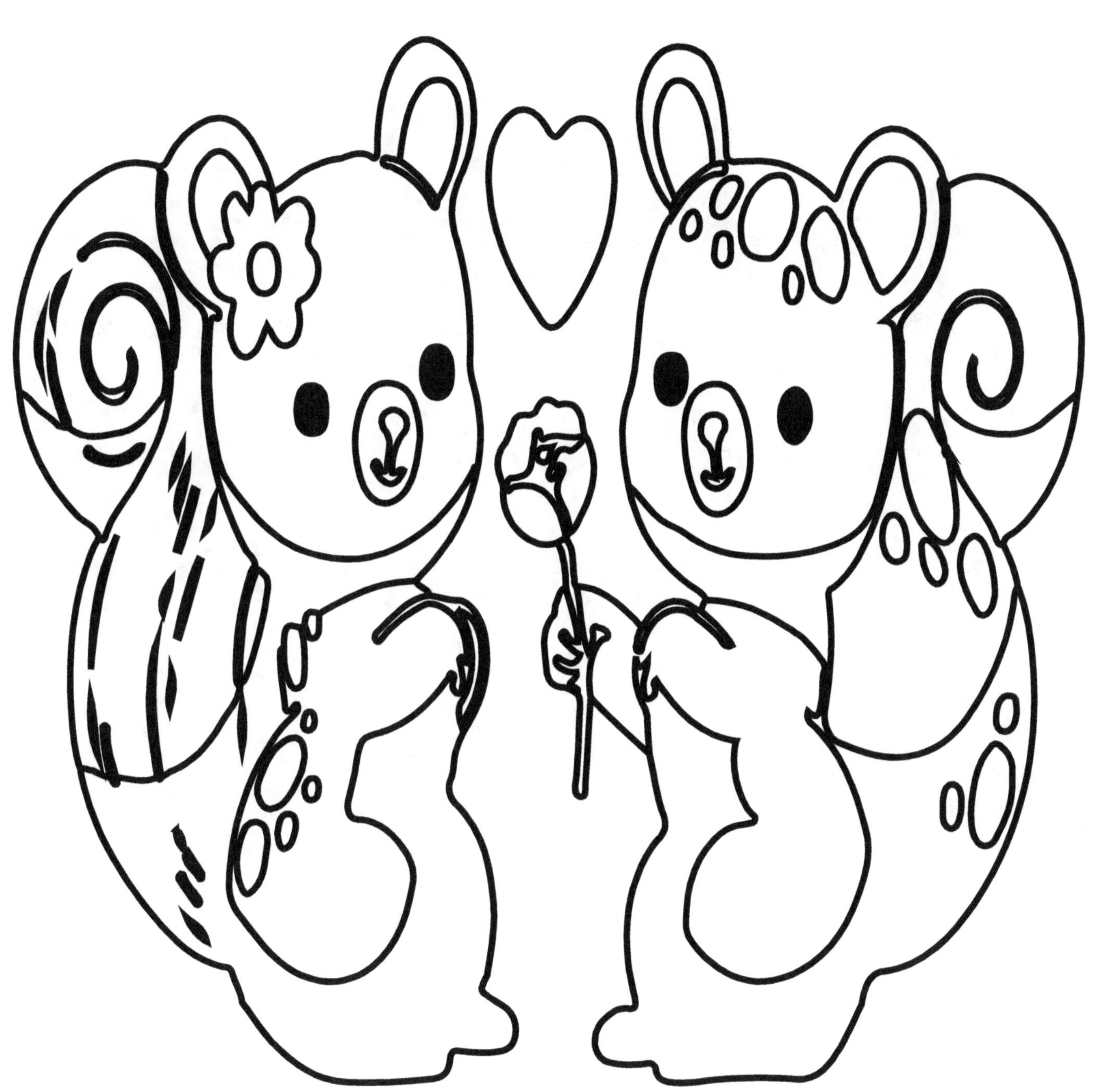

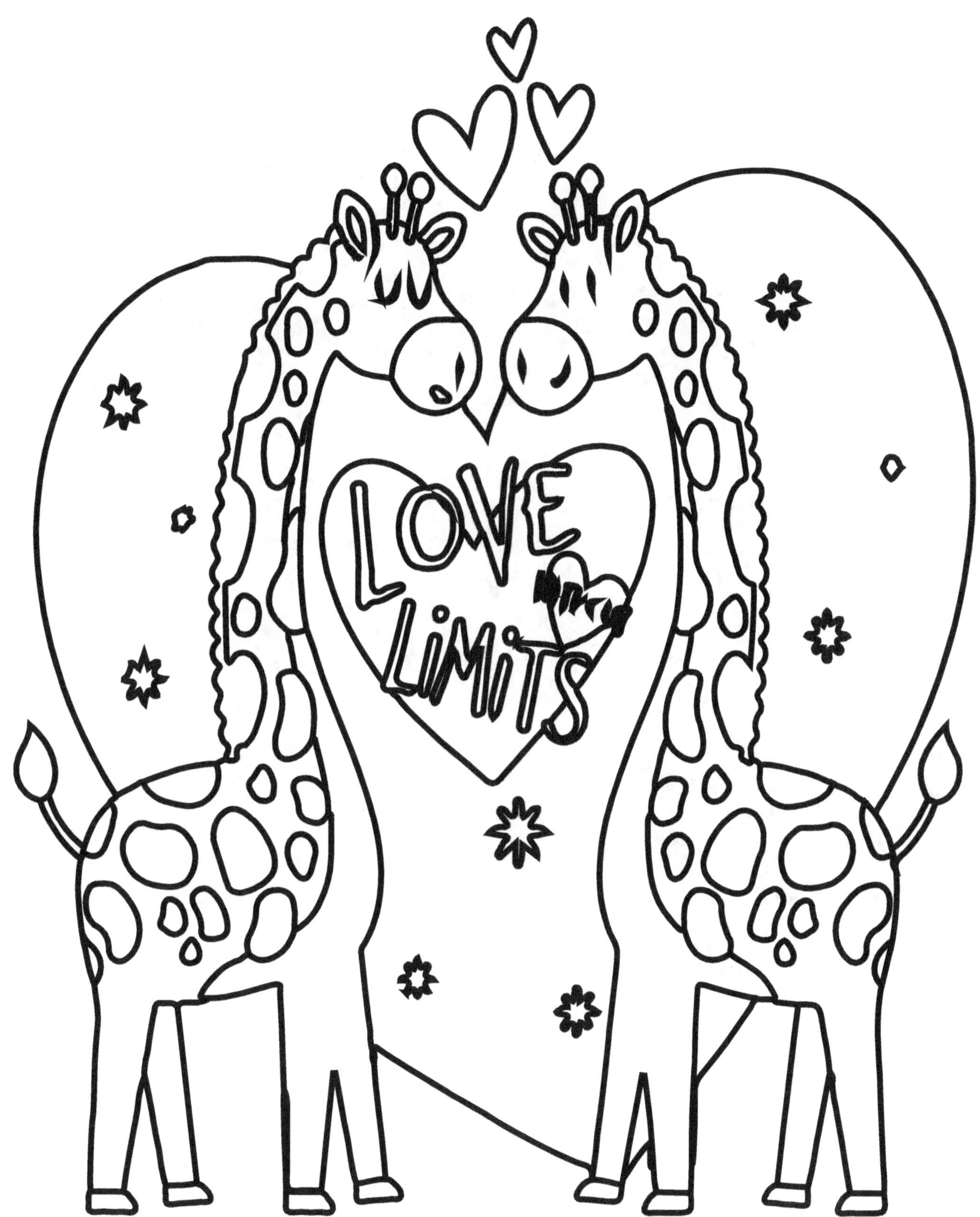

LOVE
LIMITS

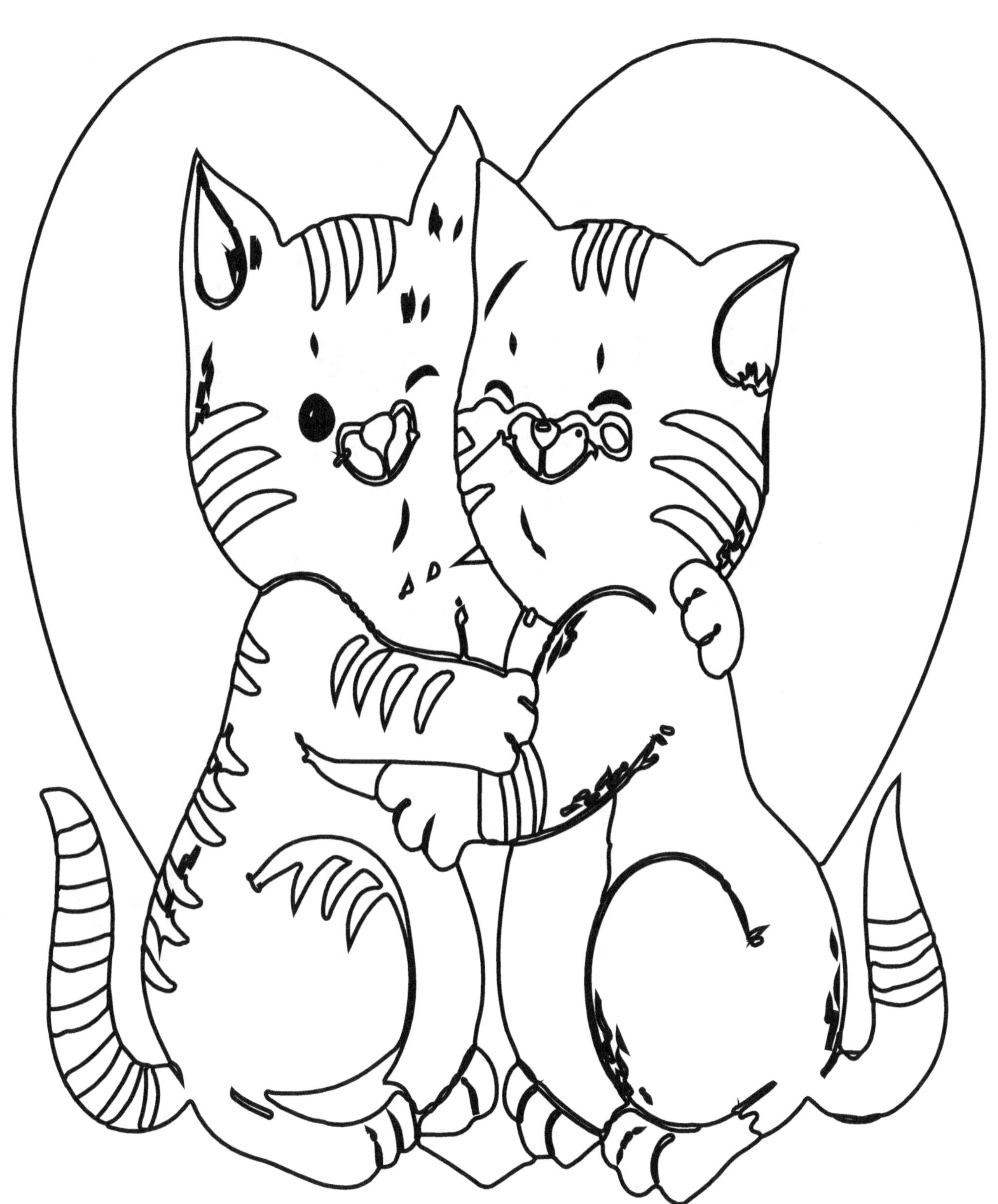

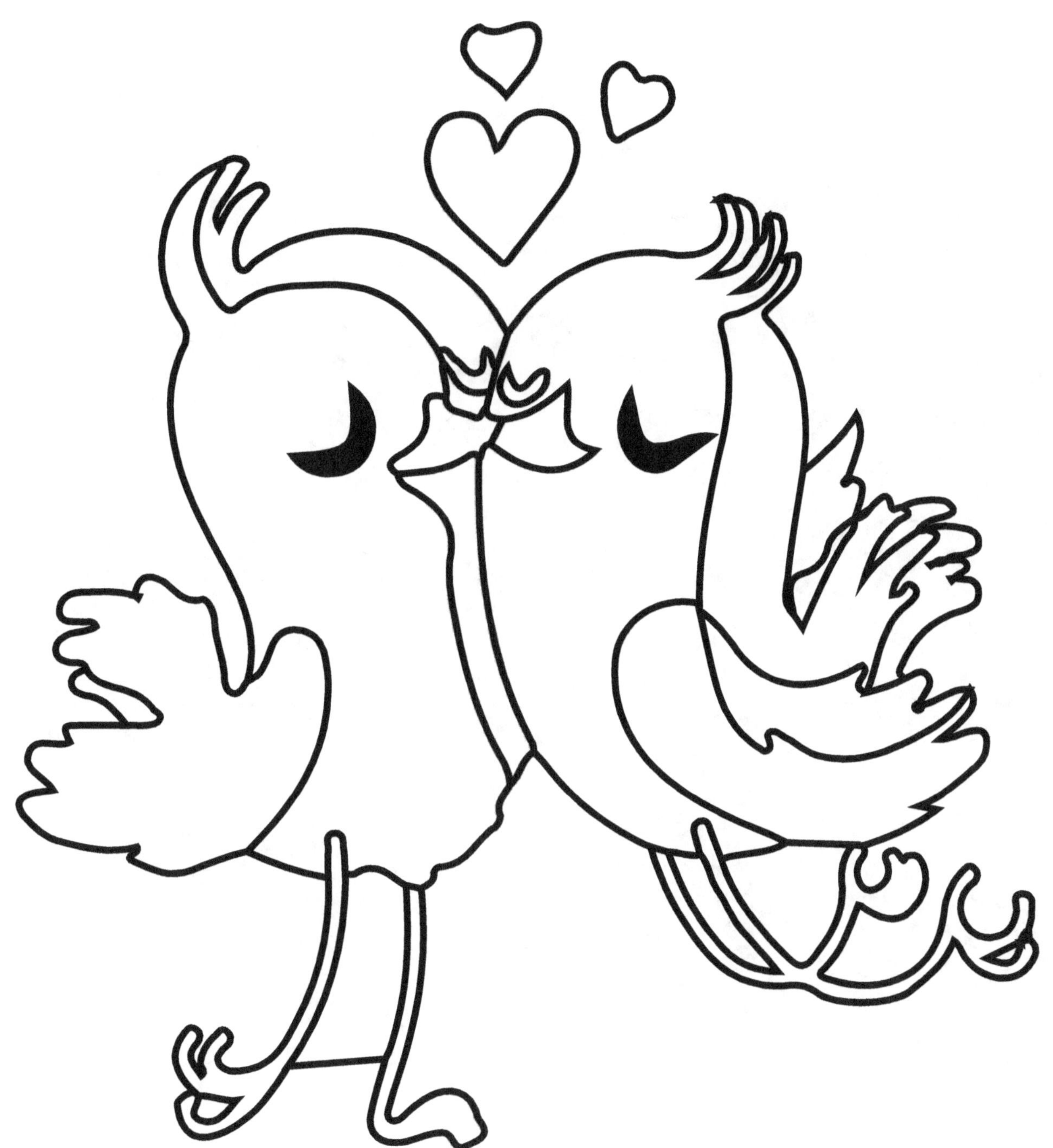

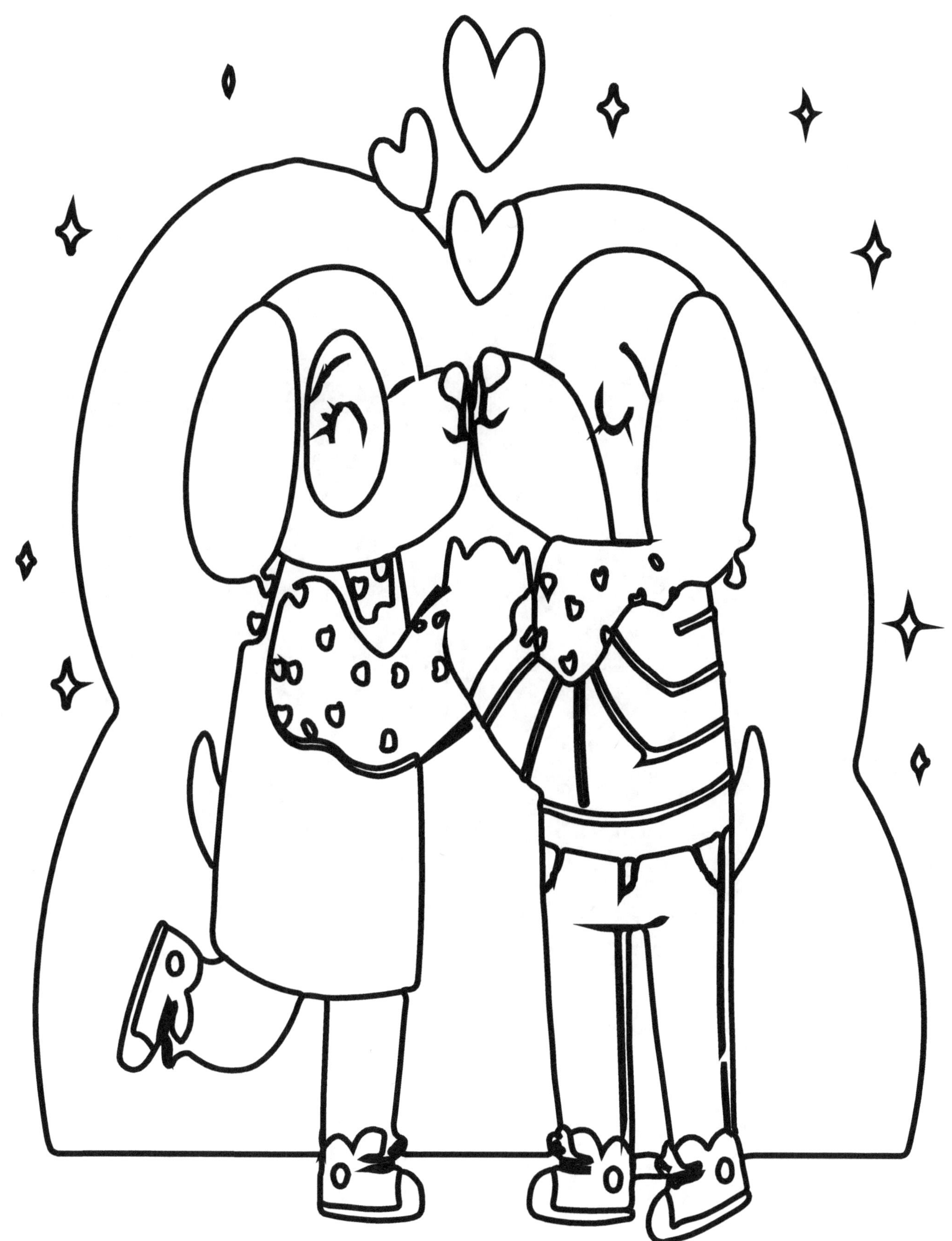

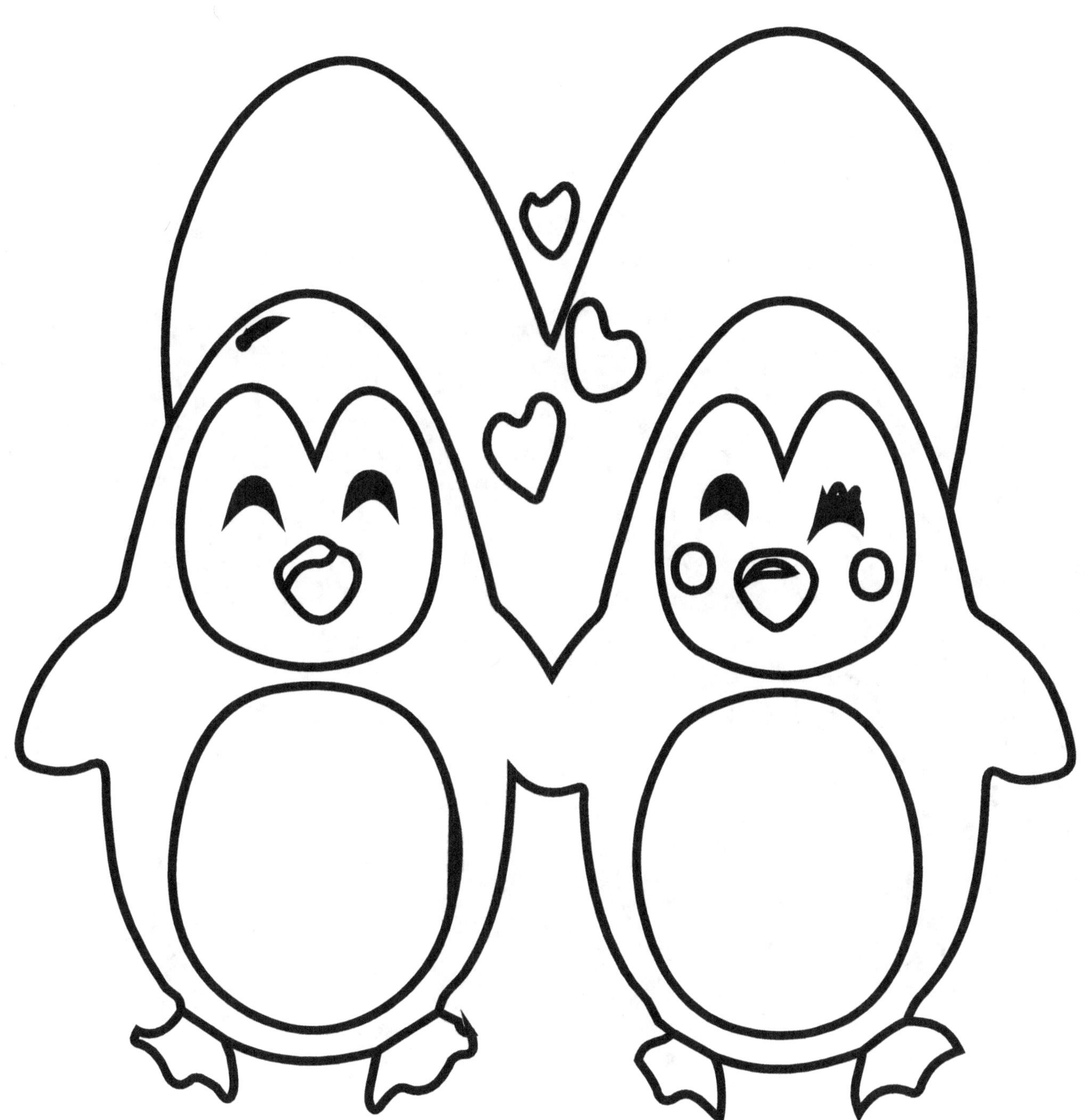

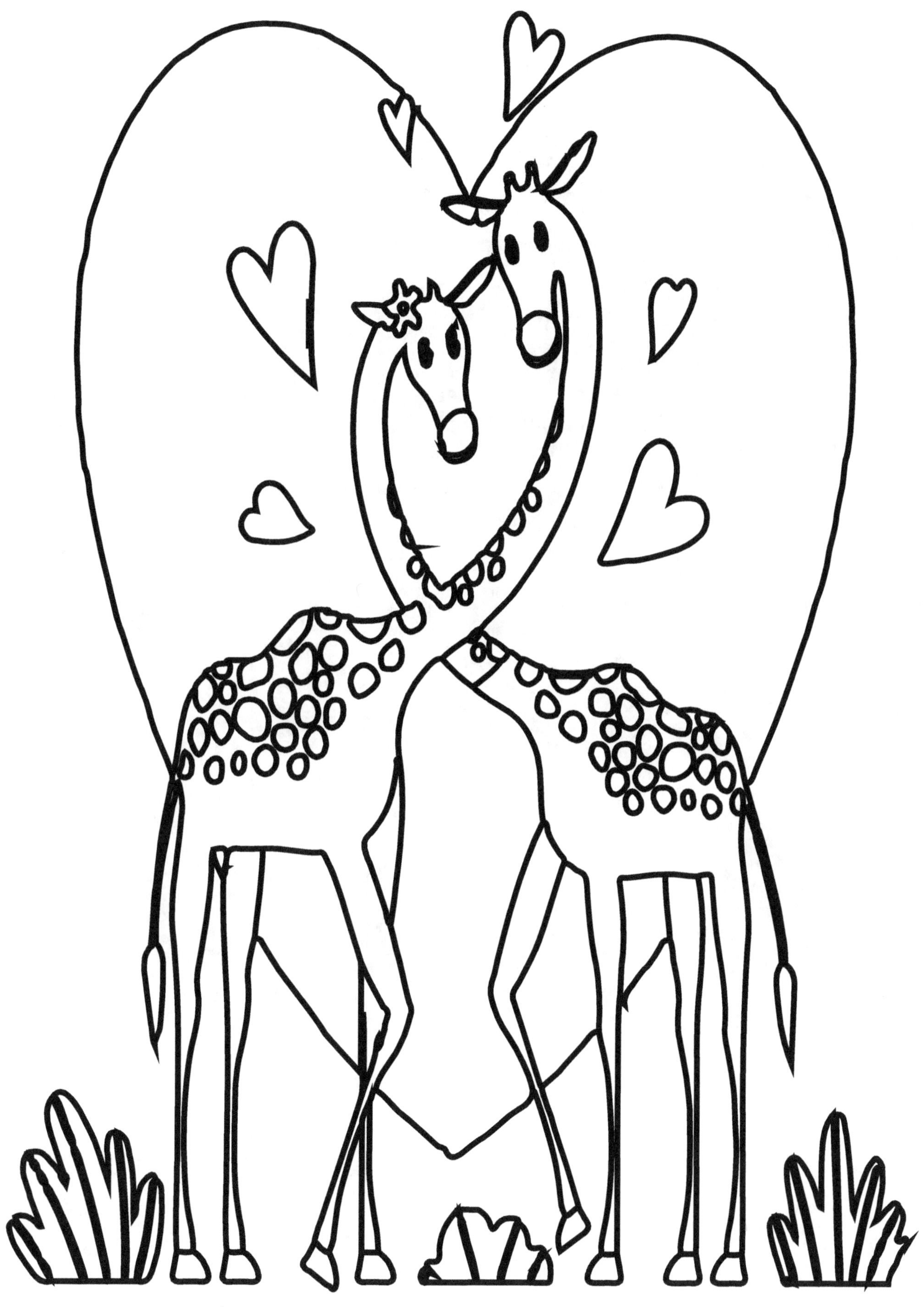

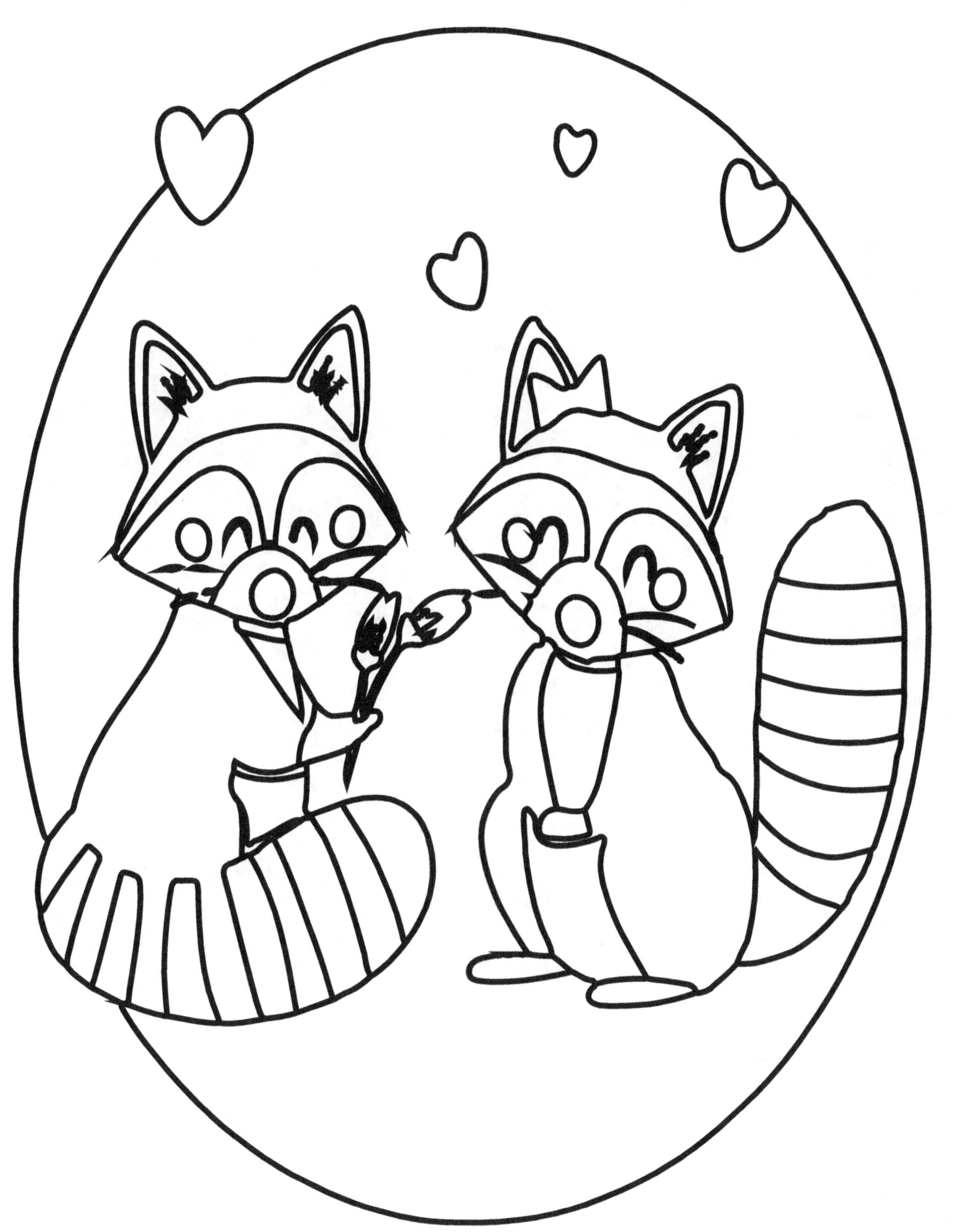

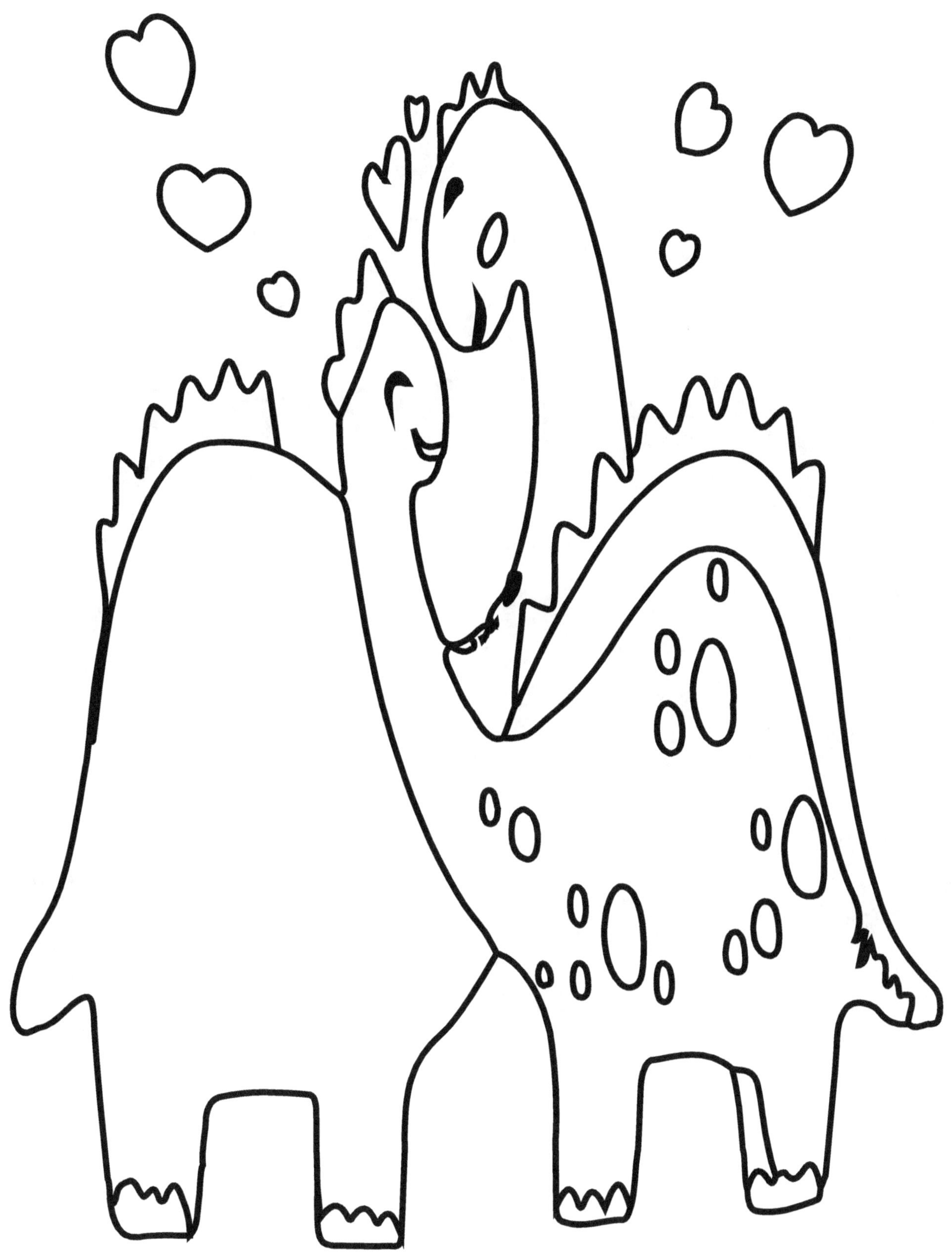

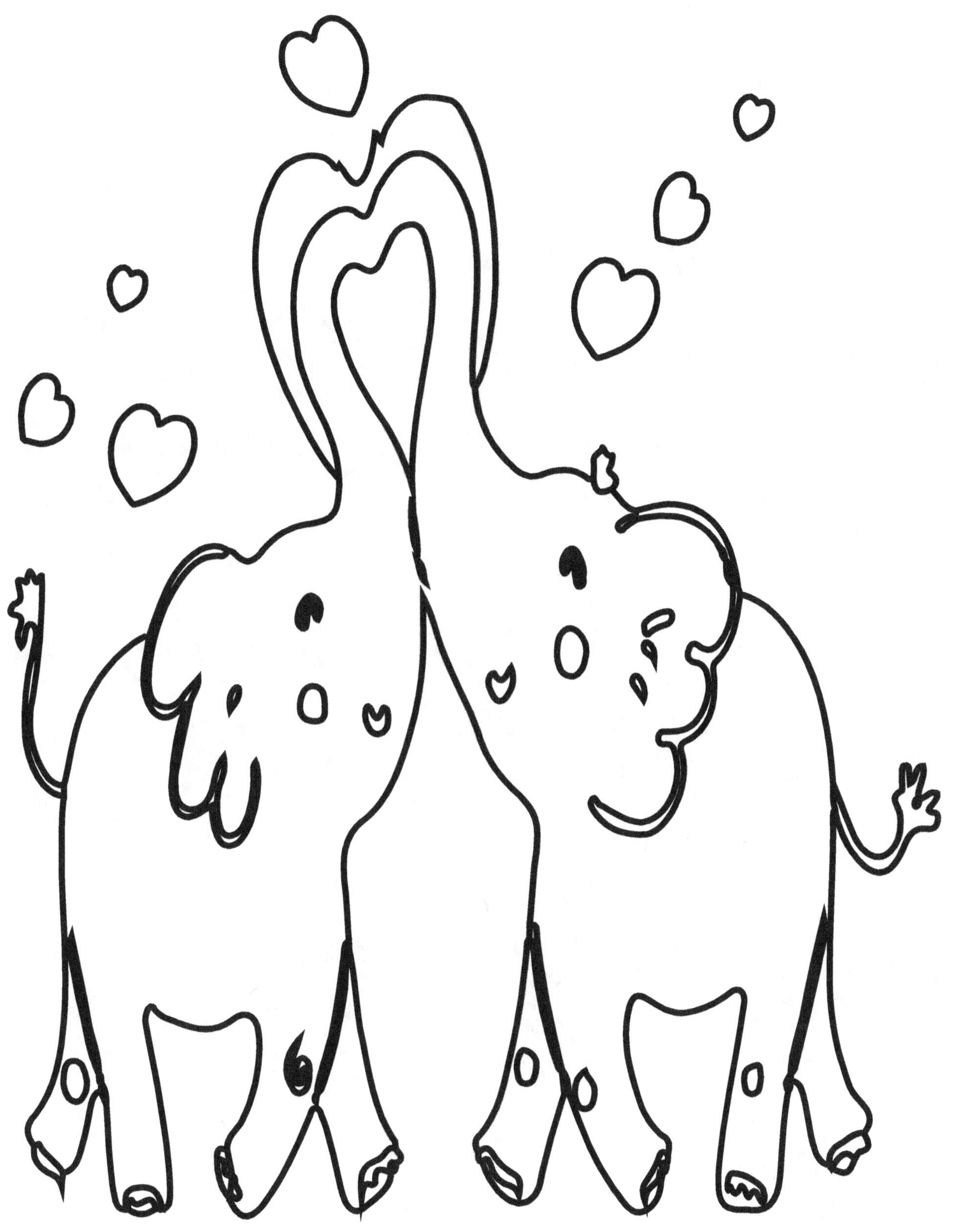

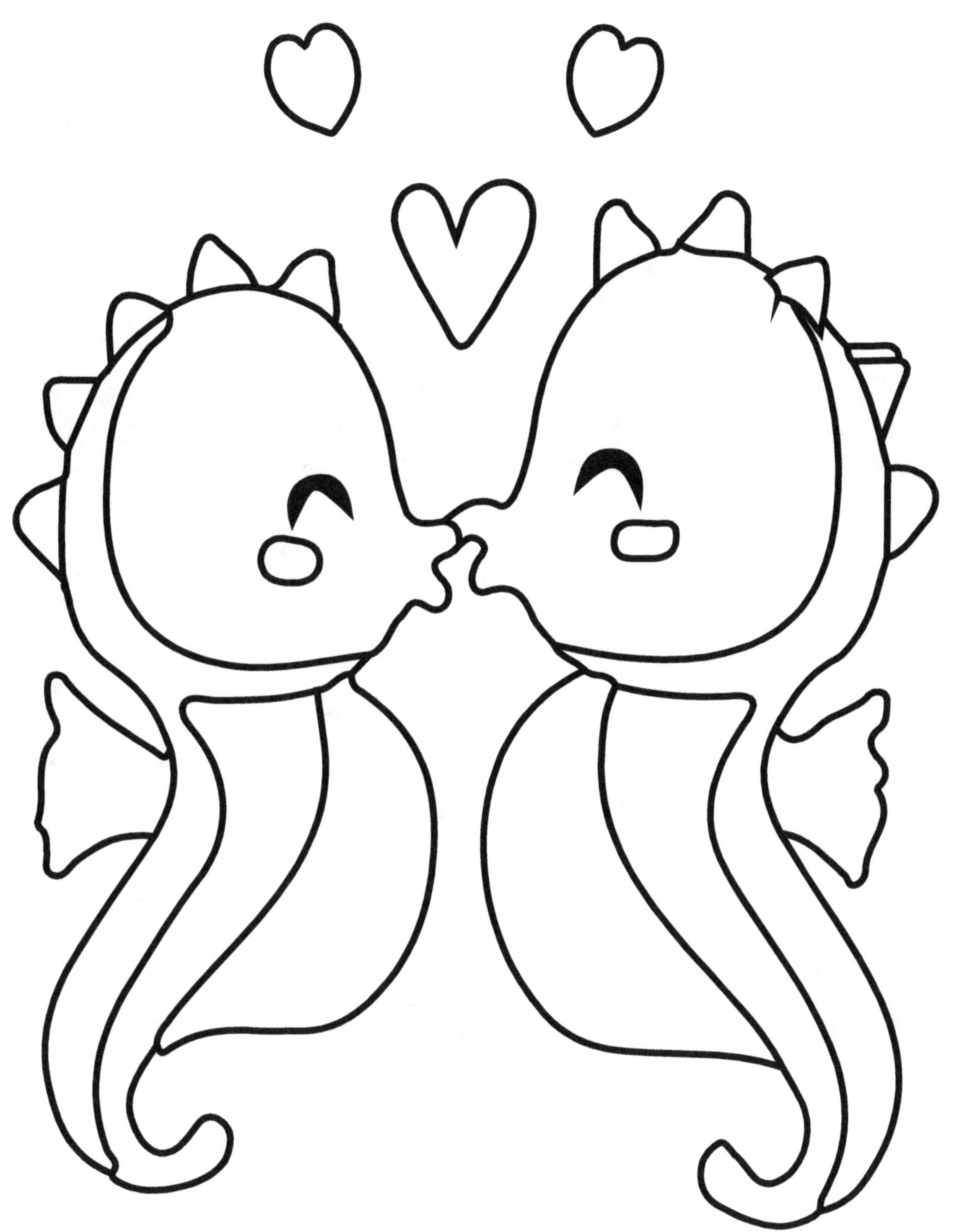

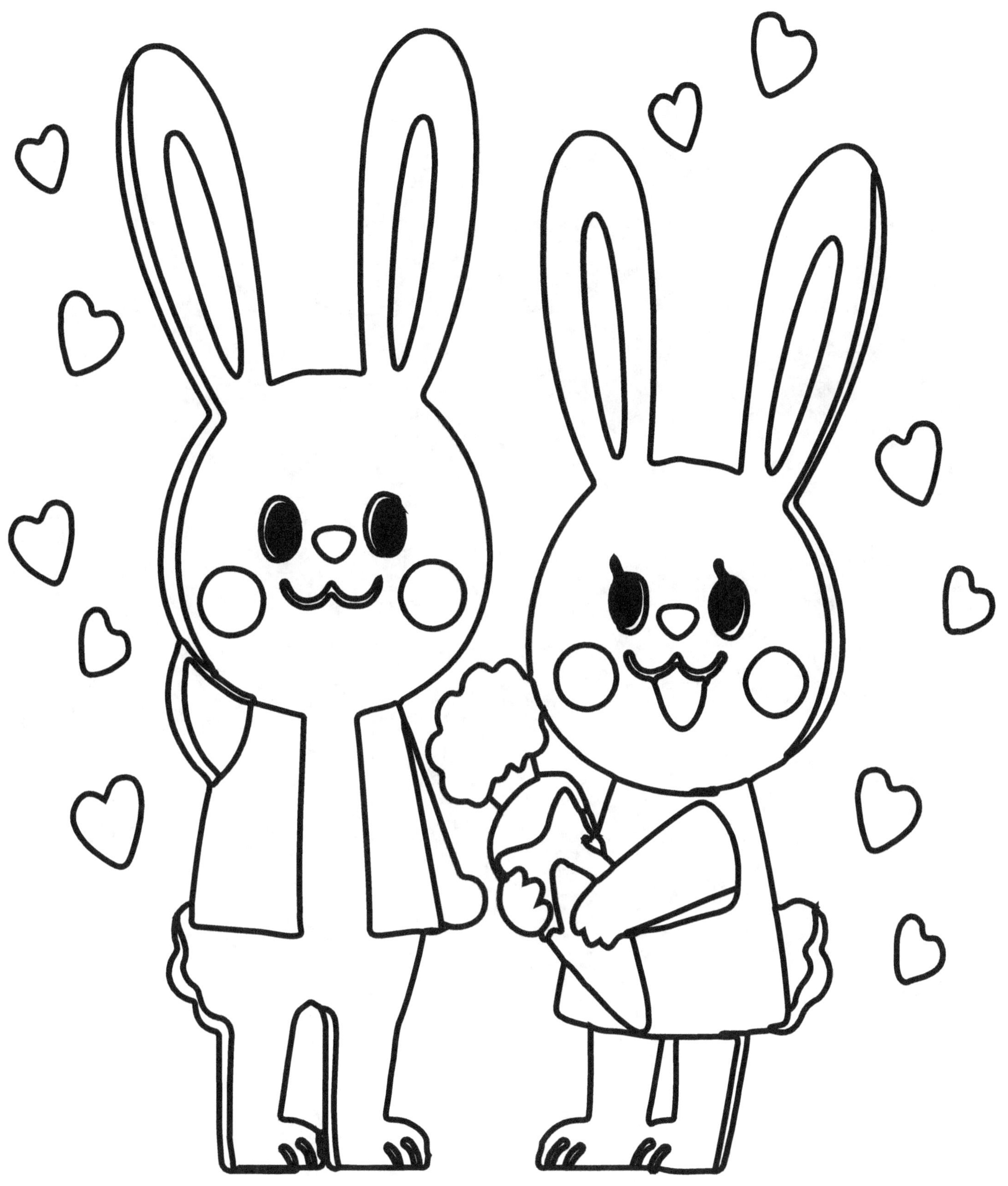

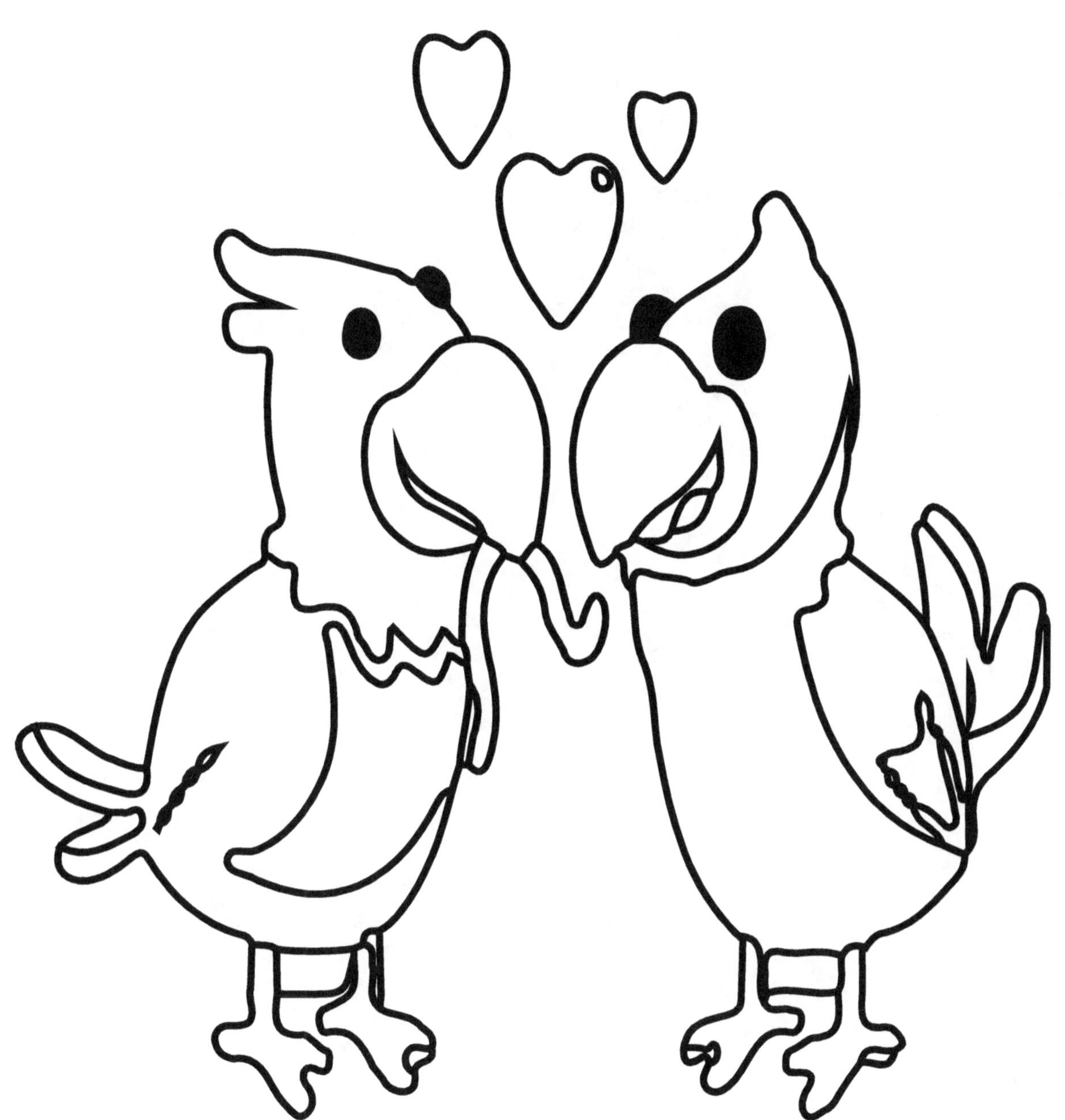

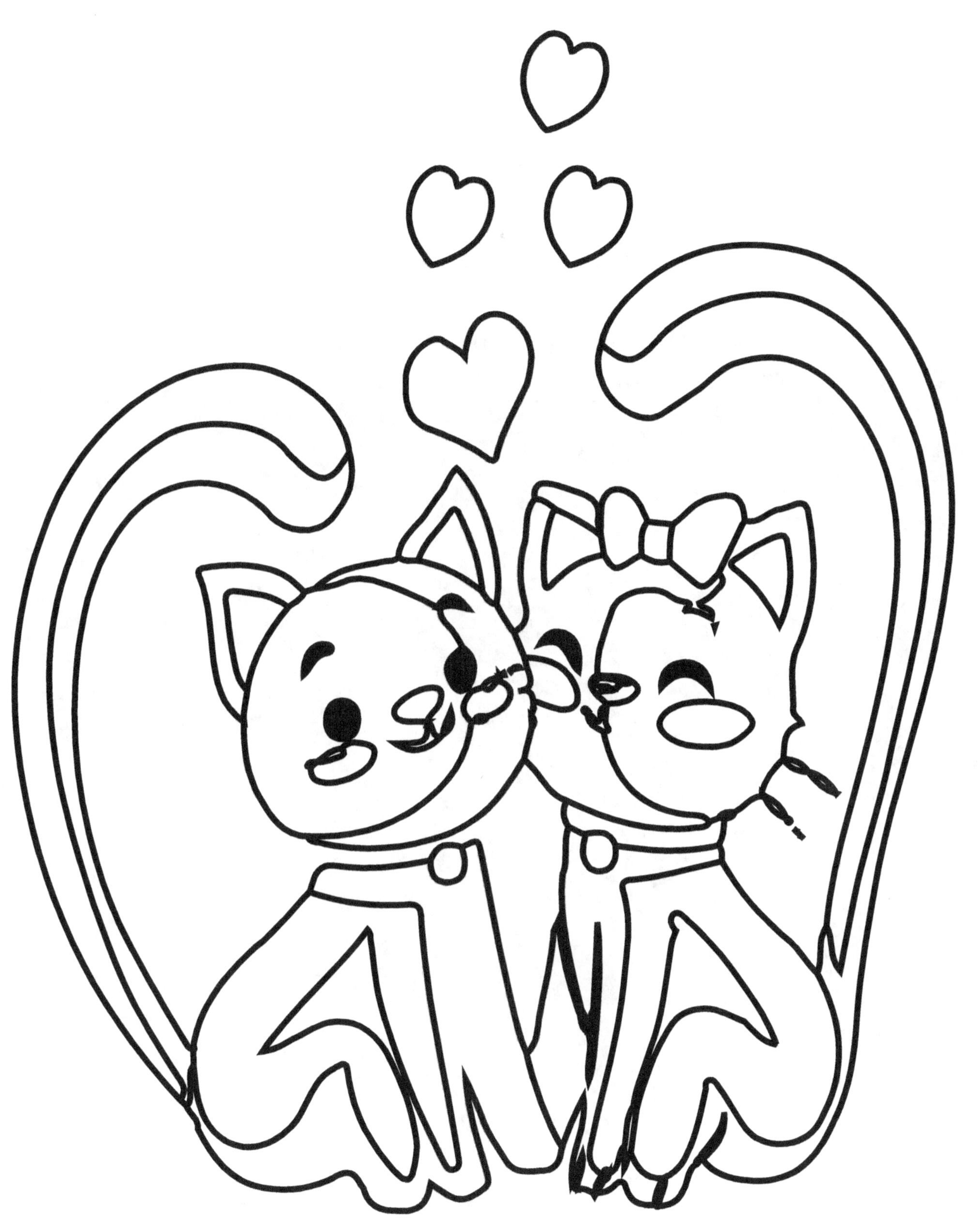

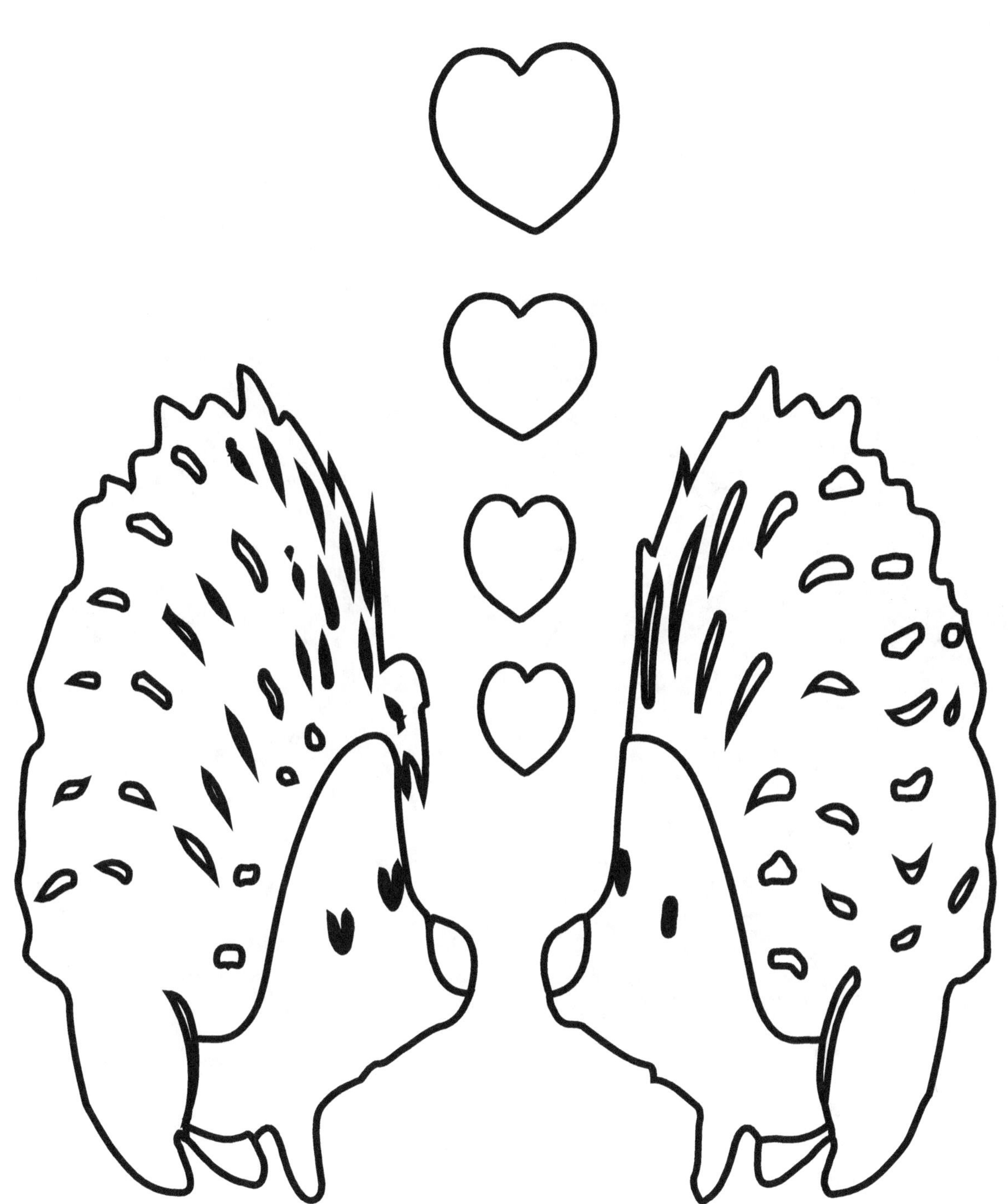

Please take a couple of minutes to leave us
a Review and Rating !!!

Thank you and good Luck !

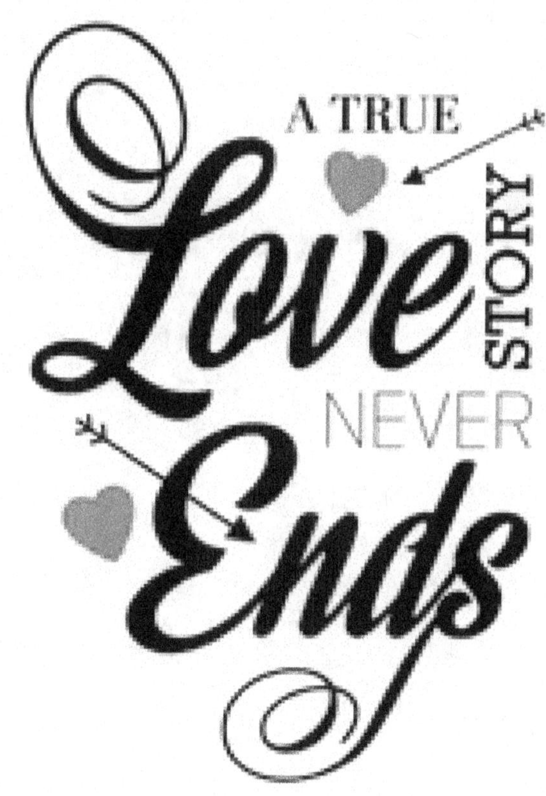

image credits to : freepik.com